✤

COPTIC ORTHODOX
PATRIARCHATE

See of St. Mark

WORDS

OF

SPIRITUAL BENEFIT

101 - 150

(Volume Three)

BY
H. H. POPE SHENOUDA III

Title: Words of Spiritual Benefit (Volume 111).
Author: H. H. Pope Shenouda 111.
Translated by: Mrs. Basilius, Australia.
Revised by: Mrs Wedad Abbas.
Illustrated By : Sister Sawsan.
Typesetting: J.C. Center.
Press: Dar El Tebaa El Kawmia.
Edition: The second edition - December 1991.
Legal Deposit No.: 9838/1991.
I.S.B.N.:   977-00-2736-7.

*H.H. Pope Shenouda III, 117th Pope of
Alexandria and the See of St. Mark*

**In The Name Of The Father, And
Of The Son And of The Holy Spirit,
One God Amen.**

PREFACE

Dear Reader,

It is good indeed to read together one thought, so that we might all have one mind.

As I promised in the introduction to Volume II, I present you now with the third volume as part of a series of consecutive books.

They are brief concise contemplations which do not need much time to read, but need depth.

May God be with you.

SHENOUDA III

April 1981.

101- Lessons from the River Nile

Do you know that the origin of this river derived from drops of water which fell as rain, accumulated and became a river ?

Could not we learn that any major project might start with a simple thing, perhaps an idea ? It is said in proverbs that "the longest journey begins with a step".

The first sin started with a simple sitting with the serpent. Perhaps the biggest fight begins with a word.

We can learn from the Nile that the soft drops of water, if it fell orderly and continually on a rock or mountain, it can carve a way in it : an important lesson on patience and perseverance.

This water carries the clay from the mountains of Ethiopia. At the first sight it looks unclear, but it contains the silt which causes the fertility of Egypt and coveres its sand with silt.

This muddy water sings with the Bride in Song of Songs, *"I am dark, but lovely" (Song 1:5)*. In spite of such merkiness, this water carries in it good sweetness to its drinker, as the sweetness of the lives of Augustine and Moses the Black, which appeared after their repentance.

Before the cutting of the channel of the Nile, the water was flowing on the sides making swamps. But, later its channel has deepened, bit by bit, and the water became stable.

This gives us an idea on the grading in the spiritual life, and the patience of the soul until it reaches its stability after a while. We we are not to judge those who are in the "swamps" stage and have not yet reached the deep and stable channel.

We must also praise the two banks of the river (between which the river runs). They are not two barriers which limit its freedom but they are two protectors for its safe - keeping; like the Commandments, they do not restrict but protect freedom.

It is a long journey the Nile has made until it reached us, giving its riches to the countries it passed, Ethiopia, Nuba, Sudan, Egypt and all the surrounding deserts. This teaches us to give or make good to whoever we pass by.

102- The Truth

As God is Love, He is also the truth. He said, *"I am the way, the truth, and the life." (John 14:6)*.

About Himself the Lord said, *" ... And you shall know the truth, and the truth shall make you free." (John 8:32)*.

He who adheres to the truth, he adhere to God Himself. He who keeps away from the truth, keeps away from God.

Therefore, we say of the faithful that he is a truthful person.

He knows the truth, goes in the way of truth, says the truth and accepts nothing but the truth.

For the sake of truth, he fears no blame.

He says the truth, whatever the consequences are to him, as it happened to John the Baptist who said the truth and paid the price.

The truthful person says the truth even against himself, or his dearest ones; he does not treat anything with partiality.

God sent the prophets to witness for the truth in a world where evil prevailed among people. He also sent the shepherds, priests and teachers to witness for the truth.

Judiciary on earth was set to witness for the truth.

The Faculty of Law is named in Arabic "Faculty of Rights" because the word 'right' is more effective than the word 'law'.

How nice is the Bible's saying about judgement in truth, even in the normal dealings among people it said, *"He who justifies the wicked, and he who condemns the just, both of them alike are an abomination to the Lord" (Prov 17:15).*

Look at yourself; are you always with the truth ?

Are all your words true and sincere, whether in what you utter or in what you want your listener to understand ?

Do you favour any of your friends, relatives or beloved ones, and for his sake you do not mind telling the news in a way which is good to him, even if it hurts the others ?

Do you follow the truth in your practical life, principles and beliefs, and not only in your talks ?

Do you take the right of others from yourself to give it to them.

Is the truth lost in your exaggerations, jokes and justifications ?

✧ ✧ ✧

103- The Spirit of the Service

In remembering the style of our Fathers the Apostles in their service, we learn practical and ideal lessons in the spirit of service, out of which we mention the following:

1. The Warmth of the Service:

How nice is the saying of the Apostle Paul in this respect, *"who is made to stumble, and I do not burn with indignation." (2 Cor 11:29).* His saying, *" I have made myself a servant to all, that I might win the more. To the weak I became as weak, that I might win the weak. I have become all things to all men, that I might by all means save some." (1 Cor 9:19 - 22).* His zeal, in flaming love, prevailed over all.

2. Visits in the Service:

Our Fathers, the Apostles, did not establish services and leave them without a follow up, but on the contrary, they pursued their service by all means: by epistles, by disciples sent by them - as Paul used to send Titus or Timothy. Frequently, they used to make special visits, as expressed by St. Paul in his saying, *"Let us now go back and visit our brethren in every city where we have preached the word of the Lord, and see how they are going." (Acts 15:36).*

3. Service Filled with Spirit and Power:

The Apostles did not serve except after they received the Holy Spirit, as the Lord said to them*," But you shall receive power when the Holy Spirit has come upon you; and you shall be witnesses to me." (Acts 1:8)*.

How nice is the Bible's saying in this respect, *"And with great power the Apostles gave witness to the resurrection of the Lord Jesus. And great grace was upon them all." (Acts 4:33)*.

It is also beautiful what was said about St. Stephen, that he was*," Full of faith and power." (Acts 6:8)*. He stood against synagogues, *"And they were not able to resist the wisdom and the Spirit by which he spoke." (Acts 6:10)*. The nature of the spiritual service is powerful as it is from the Spirit, *" for the word of God is living and powerful." (Heb 4:12)*.

4. Service Filled with Love:

The Lord Jesus *"Loved His own ... to the end." (John 13:1)*, and with the same love He served the Apostles. It was not a mere official service.

104. Remember

✢   Remember your weakness, then you will be more cautious and you will not submit to the thoughts of pride and false glory.

✢   Remember the loving kindness of the Lord bestowed on you, and you will always be in the life of thanksgiving. Faith will grow in your heart as well as the trust in God's love and work. Your past experiences with God would be an encouragement in the life of faith.

✢   Remember people's love and their good past with you. Should you doubt their sincerity or find out they have done something wrong to you, their old love will make intercession for them and your anger will fade away.

✢   Remember death, so all worldly temptations will disappear and you feel that*," all is vanity and grasping for the wind." (Eccl 1:14).*

✢   Remember that God is standing in front of you, looking at you, then you cannot sin because you see him

✢   Remember God's promises, and you will be comforted in all your troubles. But, if you forget them, say with David the Prophet, *"Remember the word to your servant, upon which you have caused me to hope. This is my comfort in my affliction. For your word has given me life." (Ps 119:49-50).*

✣ Remember the Blood of Jesus which was shed for your sake and you will definitely know the value of your life; it becomes dear in your eyes, so you will not waste it with prodigal living, *"for you were bought at a price." (1Cor 6:20).*

✣ Remember the vows you made to God at the Baptistery, which your parents undertook on your behalf; to renounce the devil, all his evil deeds, all his thoughts and tricks, all his forces and powers.

✣ Remember always that you are a stranger on earth and that you will return to your heavenly home: then you will not put all your hopes in this world.

✣ Remember that the narrow gate leads to the kingdom of heaven. If you see the wide gate open before you, escape and keep away from it, as all those who go in by it, have perished.

✣ Remember your eternity and work for it at all times.

✣ Remember that you are a child of God, and ought to have His image. You walk as is fitting for the Children of God who are apparent.

✣ Remember that you are the temple of the Holy Spirit, and do not grieve the Holy Spirit of God in you. Be always a holy temple.

✣ Remember all what I said to you on this page and if you have already forgotten, please read it again.

105 - To Keep in Mind

God wants you to keep in mind certain matters, which are important and not to be forgotten, such as:

✢   His commandments, He said to Joshua, the son of Nun, *"This Book of the Law shall not depart from your mouth, but you shall meditate in it day and night, that you may observe to do according to all that is written in it." (Josh 1:8).* He therefore, summed up the Law in the Book of Deuteronomy. The Old Testament was divided to be read in the Synagogues on Saturdays, in order to be remembered by the people. A copy of the Law was to be given to the new king to remind him.

✢   **In order to remind us, God set down feasts and high days to remember Him, as in the Feast of the Passover.**

✢   God does not want us to forget the salvation which was completed by the blood of the Lamb, so he made it a yearly feast.

In order not to forget His help in sending the Manna, He kept some of it in the Ark of the covenant in the tabernacle.

In order not to forget the crossing over the Jordan. Joshua took twelve stones and laid them down there, in the midst of the

Jordan, in the place where the feet of the priests stood. (Josh 4:8-9).

✥   Similarly, the church puts some facts before us to make us remember and to learn from it, for example :

The benefit of remembering God's love for us, which appeared in giving Himself for us on the Cross. The church performs a yearly commemoration in the Passion Week. Nevertheless. a Mass is performed weekly on Friday to remember the sufferings of Christ and His Crucifixion in the prayer of the sixth hour.

✥ **As remembering death is beneficial, the Prophet David says,** *"Lord, make me to know my end, and what the measure of my days, that I may know how frail I am."(Ps. 39:4).*

✥ For the benefit of its children, the church reminds them of death in the Compline, also of the coming of our Lord Jesus Christ for judgement, in the midnight prayer.

✥   Besides, in the canonical hours, in the readings as well as in the Holy Mass, the church reminds us of many things which are profitable to our life.

Sermons are reminders of matters we probably knew before.

I wish we would remember, otherwise, we will be lost through forgetfulness and unawareness.

✥ ✥ ✥

106- Nights of Prayer

Among the beautiful things in our Church are the nights of prayer.

It started as a thought among the servants and it quickly spread among the people. No church is free from it especially in the nights of Kiahk (the Coptic month before Christmas). It became an established custom on New Year's Eve.

Every church does its utmost to prepare an interesting spiritual programme for the night of prayer, to help the faithful to stay awake and keep their thoughts, feelings and hearts within the spiritual act.

The programme includes prayers from the Agpia, other prayers, hymns, chants, spiritual readings, questions and answers.

The choirs at certain churches present some of its popular hymns.

The night ends with Raising of Incense and Holy Mass. Most of the congregation partake in communion and they all leave after spending a spiritual night with God, which encourages them to request its repetition.

The idea of the nights of prayer is very old. The Lord Jesus Himself put its basis as He used to spend the whole night praying. It has roots in the Old Testament, as David the Prophet says, *"Behold bless the Lord, all you servants of the Lord who by night stand in the house of the Lord ...Lift up your hands in the sanctuary and bless the Lord." (Ps 134:1-2).*

The church laid out the midnight prayer in three divisions. The monks are used to perform the midnight prayer in the rites of Praises, but for the people to spend the night in prayers is a great evidence which shows the spirituality of the church.

While the world spends its nights in fun and pleasure, the church stays up to pray, awake with God, lifting the hearts of her children to Him. Participating with the angels and the spirits of the Saints in praising.

The martyrs and confessors - even when in prison - were spending the night in prayer. Paul the Apostle used to do so.

The prayers of all these people were a kind of preaching ; which gave an idea of the God-loving and prayer-loving heart.

It is nice to train our children to keep awake during the night of prayer. They will take an example from their parents as well as from the church and the picture will reflect in their minds and hearts.

✠ ✠ ✠

107 - Effects of Association with Others

A person is greatly influenced by those he associate with.

Easy is the absorption of their attitudes, thoughts and psychological condition.

If you associate with a person who always suspects, suspicion would soon get to your heart. The opposite happens if you associate with one who has deep faith; he might be able to plant this faith in your heart.

The one who has many fears, who always expects harm and evil, could easily spread fear among those who associate with him. As for the courageous one who has a strong heart, he strengthens their hearts and his courage and firmness flow to them.

It is enough for a group of people to have one person who very often complains, curses all situations, grumbles from everything till those who sit with him leave with hearts full of complaints and grumble!!

This shows the effect of rumours and news on people.

It is another kind of effective association, either of the thought, opinion, news or feelings that surround them.

That explains the effect of friendship, relationship and marriage. Even companionship and neighbourhood. As the proverb says (Ask about the neighbour before you ask about the house).

Therefore, you ought to be selective in choosing your friends. Outline the limits of your relationship with friends, neighbours and those you associate with.

It would be even better if you associate with those who are in a better position than you. You will be able to benefit from them, as they could lift you up with them.

Do not think that you are too bright to be affected. Very few are those who do not get affected by people surrounding them.

Many a time one talks to you and you understand from his way and thought that it is carried from another friend that you know!

Many are like a mirror that gives you a reflection of the one who sits in front of it!

Others get affected in a hidden way that shows only after a while.

Some distinguished characters could be affected by their own attendants and helpers. One member of the attendants could be the main key of the personality.

Poor is the man, who has a sensitive system that picks us quickly!
✢ ✢ ✢

108 -Seek Faith

St. Paul the Apostle says, " *Examine yourselves as to whether you are in the faith. Prove yourselves." (2 Cor 13: 5).*

The faith here is not that of the mind or just the name. It is the real faith, a life-style that one lives in God and shows in all his deeds and all his feelings. The life of faith means complete submission to God and extreme trust in His work with you and the Church.

Faith cuts a road in the sea and lets water flow from the rock. It is enough to see that the Bible says, " *With God all things are possible." (Matt 19:26).* Do you have the practical faith by which you can do everything in Christ ? Or your faith is weak and could not stand tribulations ?

If you were like that, what should you do ? The Lord says," *According to your faith, let it be to you." (Matt 9:29*). The only solution is to pour yourself before God and openly say to him : Lord, I believe, but my faith has not reached the practical level yet. My faith is like the bruised reed that You, due to your love, wouldn't break; and like the smoking flax that due to Your compassion, You would not quench. Accept me Lord, with my weaknesses. Grant me this faith, a gift from You. Do not say," I'll give you according to your faith, and do not make faith a condition for the gift.   Let faith be the gift itself.

Grant me to believe in You, submit my life to You and be at Your disposal. It is sufficient for me to believe that you will grant me faith. Isn't faith also " a gift granted from above," from You, and nobody can believe without Your blessing?

You say," Only believe". Even this faith I want from You so I would not think that my humanity has done anything without You.

I am still waiting for this faith by which I could do everything through Your grace.

I believe that You will give me, and I wish after being in Your presence, to say," I believe that You have given me."

My faith then changes from a desire and a request to a reality and a life.

109 - The Ideal Day

All our days are supposed to be ideal, following the Lord's saying,*" Be perfect, be holy."* But as a matter of practice, there could be what is called " the perfect day."

The perfect day has two directions, one negative in being far from any sin and the other positive in virtue and service.

The programme of the perfect day differs from one person to another.

Some spend that day in worshipping, praying, reading, singing hymns, contemplating and fasting, in seclusion as much as possible.

Others consider it a perfect day that is spent in doing what is good for others.

Another group prefers a mixture of the two.

Some concentrate on purity of the heart. They try their best not to sin either by tongue, thought or action; no matter what the reasons are.

Others prefer to start such a day by attending the Holy Mass and receiving the Holy Communion. Certain groups of servants take it as a practice, where they all get together and they call it " A Spiritual Day".

The perfect day is offering one's complete self, with the heart and the will, for the work of the Divine grace, with keenness for self control.

There are examples of what some practise on the perfect day :

1.   God is to be the first One you talk to on that day, by a deep , diligent prayer from the heart, "And those who seek me diligently will find me."
2.   Praying all the hours in the Agbia completely, with understanding, depth and warmth.
3.   Never uttering a sinful word, or a word that has no benefit.
4.   Do not get angry with anyone and do not anger or sadden anyone.
5.   Start every work with a prayer and through prayer, work and talk.
6.   Do your best to keep your thought pure. It would be better if you continually occupied your thought with spiritual work such as spiritual readings, prayer and meditation.
7.   Act in humility, gentleness, meekness and love with all.
8.   Respect all and give preference to others over yourself.
9.   Do not judge others, especially those who would not be idealistic like you on that day.
10.   Keep your heartly feelings pure and free from evil desires and emotions.

If the day's experiment succeeded, repeat it as often as possible.
✣ ✣ ✣

110 - The Transfiguration

The first transfiguration of our nature is that God created us in his own image and likeness.

The second transfiguration is what took place on the Mount of Tabor.During the transfiguration, the Lord Jesus Christ did not appear on His own, but Moses and Elijah were with Him, representing humanity. It is the transfiguration with which our nature will be crowned in glory.

The third transfiguration is the forthcoming resurrection, when we rise in spiritual bodies of light, like the Lord's body of glory! We will be like God's angels in Heaven.

The feast of the transfiguration reminds us of the glory that our nature will receive.

God has not deprived us from glory. He has taken us from one glory to another," *For whom he foreknew, he also pre-destined to be conformed to the image of His Son ... He also glorified."* (Rom 8 : 29-30).

In the transfiguration that is to come, we will be completely free from sin and from spiritual combats.

We will be free from the material, as we take off this body and leave the whole materialistic world. The corruptible will be clothed in incorruption," *because the creation itself also will be delivered from the bondage of corruption into the glorious liberty of the children of God,"* and, " *... eagerly waiting for the adoption, the redemption of our body." (Rom 8 : 21 & 23) "We will be free from sin when we receive the crown of righteousness". (2 Tim 4 : 8).*

This righteousness will make us forget whatever relates to sin. There would not be sin and we would not know it, remember it or fight against it. We will be completely free from it and we will live in righteousness, "in the glorious liberty of the children of God."

That illustrates accurately the saying that, *"Whoever is born of God does not sin, and the wicked one does not touch him." (1 John 5 : 18).*

We are not going to transfigure alone, but the whole city if God's Heavenly Jerusalem that had no need of the sun or the moon to shine in it, *" for the glory of God illuminated it." (Rev 22 : 5).*

Permanent joy is the characteristic of this transfiguration.

Sorrow, pain and fear, the effects of sin, will all disappear.

111- Visiting

Visiting is a kind of pastoral care. St. Paul said about it, *"Let us now go back and visit our brethren in every city, where we have preached the word of the Lord, and see how they are doing."* (Acts 15:36).

Visiting is essential for whoever is in a position of responsibility.

The bishop and the priest visit the flock and the servant visits his children. Even the ordinary faithful person sits with himself, reviewing his life, where is he going?

Visiting others means that you care about them and want to make sure they are all right.

Therefore, visiting creates a deep feeling of mutual love. You visit the one you love and the one whom you visited will love you for caring about him.

The opposite is also true; lack of visiting creates a feeling of loneliness and depression. How easy for one to say, "There is nobody to ask about me, even the Church and the priests!"

Many of our brothers were lost because nobody visited them or by the time they were visited, it was too late. Either because matters, by that time, became complicated or their hearts became void of responsive feelings, love of goodness and love of the one visiting them.

For this reason, the quick action of visiting solves problems before they become serious.

This applies especially to those who are young, weak, new or those who are facing tribulations or trials or under certain pressures and are unable to save themselves or find a solution.

There is a big difference between such a visit and a social visit.

You might visit a person without seeking to help him.

You might visit him and talk about many matters without referring to God and the extent of this person's relationship with Him. A pastoral visit means entering into one's life, knowing his problems and helping in solving them creating a deep relationship between him and God.

Pastoral care means visiting others, accompanied by God. And when you leave, you must have left God in his home and in his heart.

Let us conclude by hoping that you'll ask yourself: who needs your visit? Whom have you visited but not actually helped?!

✣ ✣ ✣

112 - The Sense of Responsibility

The spiritual person realise that his life on earth is a responsibility.

His life is a message. God will ask him how his life was fruitful, productive and beneficial to all those who were in contact with him. God will ask him about what he has done and what he could have done, but he has not.

From the formal point of view, his responsibility might be limited. As for love, his responsibility is boundless. Love has room for everyone, and is always ready to serve and help.

The spiritual person questions himself before he is questioned by God: What has he done for all those people whom he knew? Is there anyone among those whom he does not know, who needs his help; he ought to know them and offer his services.

Philip was once walking on the road and saw an Ethiopian eunuch reading in the Book of Isaiah. He felt a sense of responsibility towards him. He did not leave him till he felt the service has been completed and he led him to God.

St. Mark was sitting in the shop of a cobbler called Anianus, who was fixing the saint's sandal. St. Mark had a sense of responsibility towards this cobbler. He took advantage of this opportunity and started talking to him till he believed in the Lord and so did his household.

Both of them learned from Christ when He sat next to the well near Samaria. A Samaritan woman, who was a sinner, came to draw water from the well. The Lord felt his responsibility towards her. He led her and all her townspeople to salvation.

These three meetings seemed, at the beginning, as just passing by incidents, but the sense of responsibility turned each into a chance for salvation.

If that is the case with those who meet accidentally, how proper are the formal responsibilities of a person in life.

Fatherhood is a responsibility, motherhood is a responsibility, marriage is a responsibility and serving is a responsibility. Friendship is another type of responsibility.

Do not try to apologise by passing the responsibility to others. God is going to ask you about what you have done within your limits.

The more one's sense of responsibility grows, the more the circle of his service widens. It all happens through love, not through formalities. One even volunteers to do many acts of love.

His heart makes him keen to do it, as the Bible says, " ... *To him who knows to do good and does not do it, to him it is sin." (James 4:17).*

113 - Firmness

How easy it is for one to start a spiritual life and live with God for days or weeks then relapses and regresses backwards and then loses everything!

It is important then for the one who starts to continue, settle and become firm.

Therefore, the Lord said, *"Abide in me, and I in you."* (John 15:4).

He explained to us the importance of the branch's firmness in the vine in order to bear fruit. He praised His saintly disciples not only because they stood by His side during trials, but He said to them, *"But you are those who have continued with me in my trials." (Luke 22:28).* So He praised their firmness.

In the parable of the sower, the Lord tells us about those who did not abide, *" ... and because they had no root, they withered away ... and the thorns sprang up and choked them."* (Matt 13:6).

Therefore, St. Paul the Apostle does not talk only about the importance of faith but more about being firm in faith. He says, *" ... on those who fell, severity; but towards you goodness* *if you continue in his goodness. Otherwise you also will be cut off." (Rom 11:22).*

He also says to the Colossians, *" ... to present you holy ... if indeed you continue in the faith, grounded and steadfast." (Col. 1:22-23).* And he blames the Galatians who, *"begun in the spirit"*, but did not continue and, *" ... are now being made perfect by the flesh." (Gal 3:3).*

Many are those whom the Apostle tearfully mentioned, because they did not abide.

Some started serving actively, but did not continue!

Others fancied the idea of consecration, but did not abide!

And another group started by loving God, then left their first love!

How grim it is for one to live the life of the tabernacle and altar with Abraham, then ends up in Sodom.

Or starting as one of the twelve, then betray Jesus.

Or starts his life as a mighty victorious and a Nazirite to God and the Spirit of the Lord comes upon him then ends up shaving his hair and pulls the grinder!

Abiding in the spirit is a test for our will in the midst of tribulations. Therefore, the Bible says, *"Remember those. whose faith follow, considering the outcome of their conduct." (Heb 13:7).*

114 - The Aggressive Nature

There is a person who is aggressive by nature. He is always fighting and quarrelling and is never able to calm down.

Such a person is always ready to attack. If you talk to him, he searches for a mistake to answer back. He is even ready to answer back before he starts talking.

He always expects evil and waits for others' mistakes. It is hard for him to trust anyone or praise anyone. If it happened and he praised somebody, it would probably be part of a technique to attack others. He is never constant in praising anyone, but he soon turns against him and blame him.

An aggressive natured person has a dark outlook, an eye that criticises, a thought that contradicts and a tongue that is sharp.

A person as such has a hot temper, nervous in his actions, gets angry quickly and becomes furious, raises his voice and attacks.

Therefore, an aggressive person does not like gentleness. He considers it softness in one's nature. He does not like tenderness and meekness. To cover up his sharp temper, he praises firmness and seriousness. To be serious, in his opinion, means to always carry a frown and speak harshly.

The one with an aggressive nature does not handle matters thoughtfully and calmly, but in violence. He considers the scalpel more important than the tablet.

Such an aggressive person cannot submit to a leader or a guide. He could even attack all superiors and advisers if they do not follow his own methods.

Although he does not yield to anyone, he expects submission from all those who deal with him, even if they are older than him.

Some call the aggressive nature a fiery nature.

It is not easy to deal with such a person, even in the family circle, whether it is a father, son or a husband.

One's aggressiveness could even reach quarrelling and drubbing, even killing. In the religious sphere, one could kill through his tongue or criticism.

If you are aggressive, remember what was said about Jesus, *"He will not quarrel or cry out, nor anyone hear his voice in the streets. A bruised reed he will not break, and smoking flax he will not quench." (Matt 12:19).*

115 - Hope (1)

The spiritual person who is known for the virtue of hope is always accompanied by hope in all the details of his life, which grants him strength and joy:

✤   For repentance and purity, he always has hope, knowing God will pick him up every time he falls and help him stand straight.

✤   He has hope in sharing with God every spiritual task that he encounters.   He believes in God's goodness and protection, love and promise. This faith fills his heart with hope in His response. He is full of confidence that his request has reached the presence of God and that whatever God is going to do is for his own good.

✤   In each difficulty that he faces and for each problem, he has hope that God will save him. No matter how hard it is and how late God will be, this person has hope that God will come, even in the last hours of the night. Therefore, he does not ever lose hope.

✤   With this hope in him, he does not despair, does not know failure and does not accept the word impossible. With God there is hope, even in the smoking flax and the bruised reed. There is even hope for the barren woman who never gave birth .

✤   God is the hope for those who have no hope and is the assistant of those who have no helper. God is the comforter of those with a broken heart and a harbour for those who are in the storm.

✤   This hope gives strength that springs from God, as the Lord says, *"But those who wait on the Lord, shall renew their strength; they shall mount up with wings like eagles, they shall run and not be weary. They shall walk and shall not faint." (Is. 40:31).*

✤   It is a firm faith that does not shake because it depends on God who has no variation or shadow of turning.

Jonah the Prophet had hope, even when he was in the belly of the big fish.

✤   Hope in God gives joy, *"Rejoicing in hope." (Rom 12:12).*

✤   Hope is a driving strength for work. Hope does not mean idleness, relying on God ! Never, hope is rejoicing in the work of God. It urges one to share in God's work, with enthusiasm.

✤   Live in hope and wait on the Lord, rejoicing in Him and in His work.

116 - You Yourself Be Good News

People need the one who makes them happy and lightens their troubles with the hope that opens a window of light. It shines amongst their tribulations and makes them disappear, giving a new hope.

You too be like that. If you have a joyful word, give it to people. If you have a troubling word, postpone saying it so you wouldn't disturb others.

As it says in the Bible, *"How beautiful are the feet of those who bring glad tidings of good things." (Rom 10:15).*

Be cheerful with everyone and do your utmost to spread happiness among people.

Meet people with a gentle smile and a sweet word. People do not like frowning features and angry faces that make them lose the peace of their heart and the quietness of their feelings.

Make people happy to meet you, feeling that you bring then joy and that your arrival is good news to them.

Look how people draw a good omen and rejoice in a happy word that they read in the horoscope or fortune-book. It could fill their heart with joy and boost their morale although nobody knows the future except God. What made them happy was nothing but a word.

Look at the word Gospel and how it means Good News.

Preaching the Gospel was announcing the Good News which the Angel gave to the shepherds, *"I bring you good tidings of great joy which will be to all people." (Luke 2:10).*

Look how the Lord Jesus Christ said to the people, *"Come to me all you who labour and are heavy laden, and I will give you rest." (Matt 11:28).*

If you are unable to carry people's burdens, at least do not cause them troubles.

Look how the photographers ask people to smile before they take their photo. They want the picture to be a happy one. You too should be smiling so your face would be a source of joy for people.

Some wrongly think that religion means a gloomy face and that gloominess indicates seriousness! Religion is in fact joy. Gentleness and joy are the fruits of the Spirit (Gal 5:22).

117 - Forget What Is Behind

St. Paul the Apostle said, *" ... forgetting those things which are behind and reaching forward to those things which are ahead. I press towards the goal." (Phil 3:13)* By referring to what is behind, St. Paul did not mean sins but righteousness; to do all its virtues behind it and press forward.

Therefore, it justifies the saying, "A good man forgets all the good deeds that he has done as he is too busy in the good deeds that he is still doing."

The saints never put their good deeds in front of them, but behind them. They forget it and never talk about it. If it happened that somebody mentioned it in their presence, they change the subject so that this person would forget it too.

If they remember their good deeds, they might feel self-satisfaction about their present state and forget about the work of grace in them. As when they forget these deeds and remember nothing but God's grace that works in them, then they will reach forward, feeling that there are wide spheres ahead of them, leading to the desired perfection.

Would you forget the past completely, not only its righteousness but also its hardships and troubles. Forget also the evil which memory defiles purity of the heart. Instead of that, reach forward in positive steps towards the love of God and towards eternity.

Poor are those who limit their thoughts to the past with all its troubles, mistakes and its sweet dreams. There would not be any time or strength left for them to do something for the future.

They talk about the beauty of the past, the greatness of the past, either a boosting talk or a sorrowful talk. As for the present, there is nothing about it, it does not exist, the same with the future ... etc.

The beautiful past is not going to satisfy you if the present is troublesome. Therefore, do not live on sweet memories but reach forward. Let your present always be better that your past.

Do not remember from the past except what could make your present better and gives you a push forward in repentance or in growth.

118 - The Contrite Prayer

There many qualities for the spiritual prayer. One of these qualities is to pray with faith and contrition, with understanding, concentration, love, depth and warmth. It is a prayer from the heart, not only from the lips. We would like to talk now about praying with a contrite heart.

✣   *"The sacrifices of God are a broken spirit, a broken and a contrite heart." (Ps 51:17)*

God never reject the contrite. The contrite prayer of the tax-collector was accepted before God. So the tax-collector was forgiven though his words were few only one sentence.

✣   **The contrite prayer is a prayer that confesses its sins and its unworthiness.**

There is no self-justification in such a prayer, no excuses but confession that it deserves judgement. It is a prayer in which the tax-collector did not dare to lift up his eyes and humbly stood afar.

✣   **The contrite prayer could, sometimes, be accompanied with tears.**

It is like the prayer of Hannah, the mother of Samuel. It is like Peter's tears after he denied the Lord. These tears should not be artificial or fake. It should not also be a matter of boosting that makes oneself great in his eyes or the eyes of others.

✢ The contrite prayer thanks more than seeks. It sees its unworthiness to ask for anything, or he could be ashamed of his sins so one would not dare to ask for anything except God's mercy. It is a prayer that thanks for everything, with a feeling that one deserves nothing.

✢ The contrite prayer is at the same time a solemn prayer.

In prostration, it is not only the head that clings to the dust, but it says with the psalmist, *"My soul clings to the dust." (Ps 119:25)*

It is a prayer that stands in reverence before God, talk to Him in respect, understanding and in humble words.

✢ **The contrite prayer is a prayer of dust and ashes.**

It is the prayer of one who sees himself as nothing more than dust and ashes. Like Job and the trials (Job 42:6) and our father Abraham (Geneses 10) and Nehemiah in his humility, tears and confession (Neh. 1).

"Who am I Lord to talk to You?! It is a great modesty from the Lord of Lords to listen to dust."

119 - Do Not Resist Evil

In the sermon on the mountain, the Lord said, *"But I tell you not to resist an evil person." (Matt 5:39)*. That was said in the case of an attack, so one should not revenge for himself. On the same matter, St. Paul the Apostle said, *"Repay no one evil for evil. Do not avenge yourselves." (Rom 12:17-19)*.

The Lord Jesus Christ stood silently before the Sanhedrin and before Pilate, without defending himself; while if He did, He would have convinced them all. But, *"He was led as a lamb to the slaughter, so he opened not his mouth." (Is. 53:7)*.

His refusal to resist puzzled Pilate, so he said, *"I have found no fault in this man." (Luke 23:14)*. Joseph the righteous, was cast into a pit by his brothers and he did not resist. He was sold as a slave and did not resist. Even when Potiphar put him in prison, he did not resist. He was strong in the heart by his non-resistance. As for God in Heaven, He saw and witnessed and it was all recorded.

The righteous Abel did not resist his brother Cain.

David the Prophet did not resist Saul.

In the act of non-resistance there is reliance on God the Almighty.

In most cases of resistance, there is self-reliance.

The one who does not resist evil has the virtue of endurance inside him. He also has the virtue of patience and the faith in God's action and interference.

In his silence, there is submission to God's will.

Mostly, the one who resists could easily be agitated. He gets excited quickly, reacts quickly and answers back quickly. He also quickly loses his love to the one who upset him.

The non-resistance of evil needs strong souls; strong in faith and strong in endurance.

Would you train yourself to attain this virtue.

Not to abstain from resisting and wait for God to revenge for you ! But to remain silent and forget the offence.

You do not react on the outside and even on the inside, you train yourself to remain calm without being upset.

Lift up yourself above the offence and lift up your heart to God. Do not defend because God alone is your defender.

120 -Friendship

Your true friend is the one who is sincere in his love.

The one whose love does not have hypocrisy, pretence, artificiality or doubt. All his feelings are completely true and real.

✢   **friend is also a righteous person.**

The true friend is the one who helps you to attain purity of the heart, love God and strive for your eternity.

As for the one who joins with you in committing sin, he is not a true friend; he is a partner in a life that is far from God.

Therefore, there is a difference between a friend and a companion.

The two qualities could be found sometimes in one person. But, a person might accompany you without becoming your friend. He is just a companion.

✢ **The true friend is the one who is trustworthy with your secrets.** As St. John Chrysostom says, "Let your friends be a thousand, and he who keeps your secret, one of a thousand."

✠　　**Your friend is your second heart; he could feel what you feel.**

He deeply suffers for your suffering and deeply rejoices for your happiness.

He is a stock of love and support especially at the time of need; he never deserts you.

What a beautiful saying of Wise Solomon in the Book of Ecclesiastes, *"Two are better than one, for if they fall, one will lift up his companion. But woe to him who is alone when he falls, for he has no one to help him up." (Eccl 4:9-10).*

The one who does not lift you up could not be your friend.

✠　　**Your friend is not the one who is courteous to you but the one who loves you.**

He is not the one who wins your content by agreeing with whatever you do, no matter how wrong it could be. Your friend is the one who truly loves you, wishes you good and saves you from yourself and, if necessary, saves you from your wrong thoughts.

Therefore, the Bible says, *"Faithful are the wounds of a friend, but the kisses of an enemy are deceitful." (Prov 27:6).*

✠ Your friend does not treat you in a similar way, an inch for an inch. He tolerates you in your anger and shows long suffering when you err.

His love does not change no matter how yours or his circumstances change.

121- Wheat & Tares

God sent you to earth to spread goodness. As for the evil that is on earth, leave it and do not resist it.

It is a wise policy that the Lord gave us in the parable of the tares in Matthew 13. His servants asked him, *"Do you want us to go and gather them up? But he said "No, lest while you gather up the tares you also uproot the wheat with them. Let both grow together until the harvest." (Matt 13:28-29).*

The tares remained on earth and the Lord allowed it not only to stay but to grow and grow till the harvest. It is not for us to gather it.

As for you, are you getting tired of pulling the tares while it is still on earth. You have probably lost your spirituality in doing this. What have you gained for yourself.? Maybe you found out that your wheat was uprooted with it or it became like the tares or become like it!! in anger and the loss of peace, and perhaps in losing some love!!

If you get tired, come and let us both grow wheat together; sow the seeds of love everywhere. Let us plant new seeds and water them with the living water and pray that God may make it grow. Let us ask Him in our prayers and Masses to raise it to its measure according to his grace and to grant a cheerful touch unto the earth, water it and increase its harvest.

Sow seeds of goodness everywhere. Do not be troubled if some of it fall on stony places or among the thorns. Forget all that and rejoice in the few seeds that fell on good soil and grew. This is your portion from all your toil. It is also the portion of God.

Do not waste your time, your nerves or your spirituality in uprooting evil from earth, but be positive in making good deeds.

How beautiful is the saying, "Instead of cursing the darkness, light a candle."

Light does not struggle with darkness. The presence of light is enough to make darkness disappear.

122 - Evaluation and Care

Your concern or lack of care about every matter depends on your evaluation. This shows that evaluation is of great importance.

For example, if you neglect praying, this would be an implied confession that you do not care about prayer. Whether it is the prayer that solves your problems or as means of expressing the love that exists between you and God.

Do not deceive yourself and do not try to defend. This is the truth.

As long as you put prayer last on your list - if there is time left you'll pray and if not you wouldn't - without feeling of loss or danger. If that is the case and prayer does not receive your attention, then its value in your opinion is little. Therefore, in your life, you undoubtedly depend on human hands and not on God!

If you ask me: What can I do to pray? Do I force myself? I will say that it is more important for you to feel the value of prayer, for your life on earth and for your eternity.

The same applies to other matters.

Your evaluation of people's feelings makes you care about the way you deal with them and the style and words you use when talking to them.

Your evaluation of the importance of friends and the interest in gaining people makes you care about them so you would not lose any, and to achieve this, you endure and sacrifice.

Your evaluation of eternity and its importance makes you act properly in your life on earth; you try not to sin so you would not lose your eternity.

When you sin, it proves that eternity at that time has no value in your opinion.

Your evaluation of time decides the way you are going to spend it.

The one who spends his life in extravagance, dealing with trifles, he is the one who admits that time has no value in his life.

Your evaluation of sins, the way you divide them into big ones and small ones, makes you think little about the small sins and your conscious would not trouble you when committing or confessing them.!

Would you reconsider your evaluation of many of these points.

Perhaps there are serious matters which you consider easy in evaluating them.

123 - Practising Prayer All The Time

You cannot reach at once what the saints attained in several years. Therefore, you need to follow these gradual steps:

1 - Decide, for yourself, on a short prayer that suits you. You may repeat it several times, in depth, expressing your personal feelings.

2 - Use this prayer in your leisure time to keep yourself busy without allowing your thoughts to wander over trifles or sins. That is how you can gain a double profit : praying and also resisting evil thoughts. At the same time, you use your time in what helps you spiritually.

3 - Keep your mind busy with prayer while you are among people whose talk has nothing to do with your salvation. You do not benefit from it and, at the same time, you'll be embarrassed to withdraw from them. At least, be there physically but, as for your heart, keep it busy with God in prayer without anybody noticing.

4 - You may also busy yourself with these prayers during the time you spend in public transport or waiting for it, or while you are waiting for somebody. This could also save you from worry and boredom.

5 - You may repeat these short prayers while you are sitting on the table to eat. It feeds your spirit while your body is receiving its food. At the same time, you'll keep table-manners.

6 - If anyone talked to you during these prayers, do not ignore him by remaining silent and getting yourself into trouble. Answer him briefly and quietly, then go back to your prayers.

7 - You may also repeat these prayers while you are in bed before you go to sleep. This will keep your subconscious busy with spirituality, beside the work of prayer. By doing this, your bed will be sanctified and your dreams become pure.

8 - When you wake up, start also by repeating these prayers, even before washing your face. That will make your first thought spiritual and the first one you talk to is God.

9 - Whenever you find a chance to pray, take advantage of it. That is how you overcome the problem of " wasting time " and get used to prayer.

10 - All these prayers do not prevent the Agbia prayers or your personal prayers, when you stand in reverence before God.

124 - Your Relationship With The Holy Bible

✢   Your relationship with the Holy Bible centres around : owning the Book, accompanying the Book, contemplating on It, studying and learning It and, above all, doing what is in It and training yourself to follow its commandments.

✢   To own the Bible does not mean to keep it as a rarity on your desk but to be for your continual use. You accompany it wherever you go, in your pocket or in your hand-bag. That makes it easy for you to read in it at all times.

✢   It is better to read the Bible on regular basis. It must be daily. And it is better to read extracts every morning to give room to your thoughts and meditations during the day. It fills your mind in your comings and outings.

✢   Let your readings in the Bible be with understanding, depth and contemplation. Would it be accompanied by prayer, so you would say with David," Open my eyes that I may see wondrous things from your Law."

✢   Let your reading be with a solemn spirit so you would benefit from it . Remember how we stand at Church in great reverence to listen to the Holy Gospel. Beware of reading in negligence or a stray thought.

✛   What is important is not the amount of what you read but the depth in reading. That is when the Lord's words penetrate deep in your heart and make it touch your feelings.

✛   Try to learn some verses that represent certain principles or especial effect or some of God's promises and answers to matters that bother you.

✛   Repeat these verses in your heart many times in a manner of enjoyment that makes them stick to your spirit and depths.

✛   Look at these verses from the practical side. Make it a subject for your spiritual training. That is how you transform the Bible into life and it becomes part of you.

✛   Do not be literal in your reading but spiritual. If you need help, there is nothing wrong in asking.

✛   The important thing is to receive a spiritual benefit from reading.

125 - The Element of Memorising

One of the useful practices during fasting is to practise memorising. We mean memorising psalms, prayers, chants and hymns. It could also be memorising verses and extracts from the Bible.

By memorising, you keep yourself busy with something that is useful spiritually.

By memorising, you plant in your subconscious and in your memory spiritual matters that could be of benefit to you later on, when you remember them.

By memorising, you feel you are in a spiritual atmosphere, just like that of prayer and you get a chance to contemplate on what you learned.

By memorising verses from the Bible, you will be able to find an answer for any thought that comes to you. You will also obtain an enlightened heart in divine matters and also in religious studies. The Bible becomes inside you.

By memorising psalms and prayers, you will be able to pray all the time and in any situation and any place, even among people. There would not be any need to open a book and without revealing your prayers.

By memorising, you will be able to pray while walking in the street or while on public transport. You can pray while you are in a group of people, talking about matters that do not concern you. You sit quietly, repeating the prayers you learned. They will consider you listening while you are praying within your heart, without anyone noticing you!

By memorising, you will be able to pray in the dark and entertain yourself by contemplating while on a trip or a long walk.

As a suggested programme for memorising, one may start by the common parts in the Agbia such as the Thanksgiving prayer, the Psalm 50 and the Trisagion. Then turn to some psalms and parts, absolutions and Gospels from the seven prayers, whatever pleases one's heart.

One could also memorise some known parts from the Bible, such as (1 Cor 13) about love, or (Rom 12) or (Thess. 5: 12-28), or (Phil 3:7 - 14).

As for the young, they may learn to memorise many verses according to the alphabetical order. They could also learn some chants, hymns and Agbia prayers as far as it is within their level.

Competitions could be held at Sunday Schools and exchange reciting among friends.

✠ ✠ ✠

126 - Do Not Postpone

If the grace of God worked in your heart and felt a strong desire to repent, do not hesitate not even for a few minutes.

You do not know, perhaps the motive might cease, also the outside effect, then the desire to repent goes away and you try to look for repentance and you cannot find it.

Your deferment for repentance gives Satan a chance to be prepared for you and put obstacles in your way. When he knew of your intention to repent, his wars will become fierce and he will make it difficult for you.

The Bible considers your rejection of the voice of God, a kind of hardness of the heart. The Divine Inspiration says, *"Today if you will hear his voice, do not harden your hearts." (Heb 3:15).*

Such deferment, or the non-response to the voice of God is considered negligence of the work of grace.

God might allow His grace to be taken away from you, or deliver you to the hands of your enemies in order that you may know the value of the grace you rejected and not to refuse to accept the work of grace for repentance.

The prodigal son, when he came to himself, he said, *"I will arise and go to my father." (Luke 15:18)*. Immediately he arose and went he seized the spiritual warmth before it became cool in the heart and before it was snatched by the enemy.

The Bible says, *"Redeeming the time, because the days are evil." (Eph. 5:16).* Therefore, benefit from a time when you feel a longing for God; turn such a desire into a practical fact showing that you seek God as He seeks you.

Many of those who delay repentance, they never repented. Or when they tried to repent later they found it very difficult. What is worst, many of them did not want to repent.!

Every time you delay repentance, say to yourself what is the meaning of this? Does it mean that you forsake God's reconciliation?! Or do you prefer to continue resisting Him?! Or do you not mind the strife with God and wound his love ?

127 - How To Confess

(in preparation for the New Year)

1. First, you must be convinced that you have sinned, so that you confess that before God and the Confession Father. He who justifies himself or sees that is right in his action, naturally, he will not confess.

2. At confession, you confess your sins and not the sins of others. Do not put the blame on others as Adam and Eve did.

3. Sit first and make up an account with yourself in order not to forget.

4. Concentrate in your words in order not to waste the time of the confession father and the other waiting confessors.

5. Confession is not to tell stories but to mention where you sinned, because confession is to judge yourself before God in the hearing of the priest.

6. Mention the sins of work, thought, heart, tongue, senses and intention specifically not as stories.

7. Mention your wrongdoings in relation to worship and all means of grace such as praying, reading, fasting and spiritual meetings ... etc.

8. Speak of your wrongs in relation to the main virtues, such as faith, humility, love, gentleness and the remainder of the fruits of the spirit.

9. No objection that you make a comparison with the previous point to find out if you are in a spiritual growth, or tardiness, suspension or lukewarmness.

10. Go to confession with the spirit of repentance and submission, and wholeheartedly determined not to return and keep away from the causes of sin.

11. Make your confession day an ideal day with a special treat, either in preparation for or after the confession, taking no action that makes you lose your spiritual warmth.

12. In your decision to repent, beware of depending on yourself, but continually pray that God gives you strength.

13. After confession, the devil might contend with you to let you fall, put you in despair and spoil the new beginning that you started. Take care and pay good attention to any combat. If you fall, do not say 'no use' but stand up with more strength and true will.

14. Give more importance to fight the repeated sins.

✠ ✠ ✠

128 - I Want.

On New Year's eve, Lord, I do not want to make many promises, as with my previous experience, I know that I shall not fulfil any, or I will start but not finish.!

I do not want to rely on myself; I know my weakness. I know I have many good intentions, *"but to perform what is good I do not find" (Rom 7:18).*

The first thing I want Lord is to talk to you openly.

I want to present you my heart as it is, not as it should be. I want to put to You my weaknesses, as they are, so that with Your grace and Holy Spirit, You take charge of them.

I do wrong if I undertake that I will repent, but I cry out to you *"Restore me and I will return."(Jer. 31:18).*

I will be at fault if I promise to make many good deeds, but I ask you to strengthen me so that I can do. I want you to work in me in order to do what you want me to do, *"For it is God who works in you both to will and to work."(Phil 2:13).*

Lord, at the beginning of this year, I want you to take charge of every day in it and I want you to take this life yourself and shape it in the way which conforms with your good deed and your holy will.

I want you to uncover your will in my life. *"Teach me your statutes. Make me understand the way of your precepts." (Ps. 119:27) "Open my eyes , that I may see wondrous things from your law." (Ps. 119:18)*.

Tell me what you want and give me the strength to do it.

If I do wrong and fall, excuse my weakness and hold my hand to rise.

I do not ask only for myself but for those whom I love, as well as those whom you like most, because you chose them temples for your spirit. *"Holy Father, keep them through your name, Sanctify them by your truth." (John 17:11&17)*.

Fill them with your Holy Spirit.

I want their names to be written in the Lamb's book of life.

129 - Do Not Despair

No matter how weak your spiritual life is, do not despair, as desperation is one of Satan's wars by which he wants to weaken your morals, abolish your ability, to fall in his hands.

If you despair of yourself, never despair of the grace of God. If your deeds do not lead you to repentance, God's work for you might do.

Sometimes, in your spiritual life, the cause of despair could be the placement of ideals above your level, or taking steps which do not comply with the necessary gradual progress.

As you cannot achieve what you want, you despair.

Therefore, it is better that you put before you a gradual system in the limits of your power and abilities. Be aware that God wants only one step from you and if you take it He will lead you to the next and so on.

You might despair because you cannot stand before the Lord unless, first, you make yourself better.

It is preferable to say to Him I cannot reform myself and then come to You, but I come to You so you can make me better.

Do not despair if you feel that you do not love God. Do not say what is the use of all my works if I do not love Him!

Say: if I do not love God, it is a comfort that He loves me and with His love He can make me love Him.

If your are using the spiritual means and you do not have a true relationship with God, do not despair.

Keep on the spiritual readings, even if it is without understanding. Keep on praying, even if it is without warmth, also in confession even if it is without penitence. Perhaps because of your perseverance, the Grace of God will seek you and give you the understanding, warmth and penitence.

Your pure perseverance in the spiritual means puts God in your mind even without repentance! but if despair and repeal these commandments, you might go downwards and forget God completely.

Even if you are in a weak state, do not despair. It is better for you to stay as you are, than being pushed to the worse.

130 - The Other Half

✣   He who complains, perhaps, he sometimes produces half the truth, so he seems unkindly treated. Mostly, he does not produce the other half; the cause of such assault. He therefore does not give a complete picture of the truth. By investigation, it is possible to uncover the other details which explain the situation.

✣   An open person mentions everything - the "ins and outs" - by that he puts all the facts without hiding.

✣   He who praises himself, he too gives half the truth, i.e. the white spots in his life. There are other adverse spots - if put together - they give a full picture of his personality, character and actions.

In the same way, we speak about the mother who praises or defends he son; or the subordinate who always commend his boss.

✣   Any person who gives a bias to a certain body, or to be prejudice against an idea, course, philosophy or a trend, he mostly applies half the truth; he only quotes the good points concerning what he likes or whom he admires, but the other half of the truth could be said by the opposing side.

Prosecution represents half the truth, and defence represents the other half, and with the two together, the truth comes out.

✛   Further support represents half the truth, while the opposition submits the other half, and the full picture is complete with the combination of the two.

What you see in yourself is half the truth, and what others see in you, is the other half.

✛   The visible facts are part of the truth and the hidden ones are another part, which could be the major part.

✛   What you pronounce of your principles, ideas or aspirations is merely a part, but the other part is what you perform of these principles.

✛   Your personality outside your home and among people is half the truth. Perhaps your life with your family is another thing. Your inner heart, thoughts and feelings are a third thing. You are the three together.

✛   Until when will people live with half the truth?

Perhaps the other half the Lord will declare on Judgement Day.

131- Grace and Vengeance

How astonishing are the persons whom God gives them grace and they turn it into vengeance.

Money is grace, beauty is grace, art is grace, also freedom, science, power, discipline. But, how easy - practically - all these can be changed into vengeance's, by different means!

By the improper use, such pleasures could turn into vengeance's.

Money buys and sells conscience. Beauty becomes a tool of enticement. Art turns into entertainment. Freedom becomes means of rashness and inattentiveness. Power develops into an instrument of tyranny. Science is used in destructible and harmful inventions. Discipline - by misuse - turns into routine and an implement of delaying !!

These pleasures - by competition - could be converted into vengeance's !

In the course of competition in the fields of money or science or power or art, how easy a person contracts the hostility of his brother. Hatred and rumours spread; and struggle occurs - in which a person loses his humanity and love for others.

Nevertheless, what can I say? Even the service, the service of God !! Satan can also penetrate into the sphere of the service and change it into vengeance. If there are differences of opinion, it will turn into disputes; aspirations for improvement will change to destruction and defamation.

There will be competition for leadership as in the worldly affairs too!

As the one invention could be used for good and evil, likewise all the other possibilities.

Thus it all depends on the person himself, on the heart, mind and will by which the matter becomes a grace or a vengeance.

At the martyrdom period, persecution seemed to be vengeance, but the saints changed it into grace and they received its blessings and crowns. The bloods of the martyrs became the seeds of faith. The church grew greater in spirituality and became more attached to God and deeply involved in holiness in preparation for eternity.

Trials and diseases were changed into blessings by the saintly.

Therefore, do not say this is a grace or a vengeance, but say it can be changed into a grace or into a vengeance.

The wise heart can convert vengeance into grace, even sin !! he takes from it contrition, humility, keenness and sympathy for sinners.

132 - The Spiritual Life

✣ **It is a permanent walk towards God. It is a continual progress towards infinity.**

It is an uninterrupted effort to perfection and perfection is boundless. Therefore, the spiritual life is not meant for the one who stops, sits or sleeps. It needs a person who always go forward with all his power.

✣ **It is a transition from perfection to better perfection it is always connected with growth.**

The spiritual life does not mean that you live a good life but to move from a good to a better and a far better life with no limitation. It is summarised in one phrase said by the Apostle Paul, " ... *reaching forward to those things which are ahead, I press towards the goal.*"

✣ **Poor is the man who spends all his life to combat sin.**

It is assumed that he brings sin to an end and enters the life of righteousness, then he grows until he reaches perfection. He proceeds gradually from the proportional perfection pressing towards the absolute perfection which he will not attain the righteous feels that he is always at fault and negligent because the target before him is still far away.

The spiritual person does his utmost - which he considers not enough - Thus he widens the circle of his abilities trying to find new skills for himself.

In all of this he struggles with himself and battles with the grace in him striving with God to lead him as He guided the saints.

✛ **Do not move slowly in the way of spiritual life. Do not stop or be distracted by the sceneries of the road. Do not allow your enemies or friends to hinder you**. Tell them as Lazarus of Damascus said to Rebekah's parents, *"Do not hinder me, since the Lord has prospered my way." (Gen. 24:56).* Remember the Lord's saying," ... *greet no one along the road." (Luke 10:4).* Do not preoccupy yourselves with a relative or a friend, but repeat the saying of the Apostle Peter to the Lord, *"We have left all and followed you." (Matt 19:27).*

✛ The Samaritan woman did not want to be hindered by her water-pot, she left it by the well and hastened to the city to preach Jesus to them.

We have many water-pots, when one becomes empty we fill it again. We did not leave the well, the pots or the water. We did not go down the road and we did not preach Jesus

✛ Believe me the whole life is not enough to get across our way to God. How much is our loss; the years we wasted from our lives, which were the best of our times with more energy and greater reward.

✛   **Very often, our best times are those in which we talk about the way, its beauty and its spirituality, without walking in it!!**

Merely, we are learned and well informed, we prepare lessons and give them to the people!!

133 - Places of the Saints

What is your feeling when you visit the places of the saints; for example, when you visit a monastery for the feast of a saint?

1. The trip to the monastery is not a visit to look at or to promenade but to seek the blessing and the spiritual benefit.

2. Therefore, the singular visits are more deeper and beneficial than the excursions where many crowd together.

3. In your visit to the monastery, bear in mind all the spiritual memories and thoughts relating to this sacred place.

4. Remember that you are in a place full of reverence and silence, not noise and loud voices which occur in the cities. The saints used to keep silent and devote themselves to contemplation and praying. You too, keep silent and enter into the depth of your soul so that you can go into the depth of God.

5. Do not waste the time of the excursion in laughs and fun with your companions, in your way to and from the monastery, in order not to lose the spiritual benefit.

6. Do not make comments on all what you see or hear. Do not judge this or that lest you receive condemnation instead of blessing.

7. Remember the names of the saints who lived at that place and the virtues of each of them, meditate on their lives and their deep relation with God and what you can do to follow their footsteps.

8. Take with you a prayers book and a notebook to write your contemplations. Contact those from whom you can benefit spiritually.

9. Remember that every span of the ground was watered by the tears of the saints and that your are moving on holy land.

10. Seek the intercession of the saints of the monastery and utilise your visit by pouring out your prayers before God, asking for their prayers to support you.

11. Benefit from the quiet nature and calm atmosphere and sit and examine yourself in depth.

12. Ask yourself openly what did you benefit from the trip.

134 - The Elements of Continuance

The element of continuance is very important in the spiritual life.

It is easy that man begins a relationship with God, but can he continue or not?!

The Galatians "have begun in the Spirit" but they did not continue and concluded by the flesh (Gal 3:3). Demas served with the Apostle Paul and did not continue *"for Demas has forsaken me, having loved this present world." (2 Tim 4:10).*

How easy it is to live the life of love for a certain period. It is important to carry on as the Lord said to the angel of the church of Ephesus, *"Nevertheless I have this against you, that you have left your first love." (Rev 2:4).* And so the Lord said, "Abide in my love" (John 15:9).

Starting is easy but the strength is to continue.

If Satan finds out that you had begun a spiritual work, he will do his utmost to make you stop and not to continue. Therefore, the continuance in the spiritual work needs from you seriousness, strong will and self-control.

Continuance shows the sincerity of your wish to live with God, also it provides spiritual experiences.

If you continue with a certain virtue, you will realise its features, wars and obstacles and how to triumph over all this.

For the sake on continuance, the Lord said, *" ... he who endures to the end will be saved." (Matt 10:22)* because the good beginnings are not everything, its strength is to carry on to the end, until death.

The Apostle said, *"Remember those who rule over you, who have spoken the word of God to you, whose faith follows, considering the outcome of their conduct." (Heb 13:7).*

If you started a spiritual work and failed to continue, search for the reason. Perhaps you have begun with a level beyond your ability. In this respect the saints said, (little continuous work is better than a bigger one that stops after a time).

135 - Manners at Church

✤   You come to church with a special spiritual readiness. :

In olden times they used to come reciting the psalms on the way saying, *"I was glad when they said to me: Let us go into the House of the Lord." (Ps. 122:1) "How lovely is your tabernacle, O'Lord of hosts." (Ps. 84:1) "My soul longs for the courts of the Lord." (Ps. 84:2) "One thing I desired of the Lord that I will seek : That I may dwell in the house of the Lord all the days of my life." (Ps. 27:4) "Blessed are those who dwell in your house. They will still be praising you." (Ps. 84:4).*

✤   A person enters the church saying, *"But as for me, I will come into your house in the multitude of your mercy; In fear of you I will worship towards your holy temple." (Ps. 5:7);* so he worships and sits in reverence.

✤   Among the rules of respect of the church, it is not permissible to sit at the time when you must be standing.

✤   It is not allowable to enter the church with newspapers or magazines in your hand; the worst thing is to keep yourself busy with it.

✤ It is not permissible to raise your voice, but if you talked for necessity, you speak in a quiet voice.

78

✢   Do not engage yourself looking here and there but concentrate your senses and mind on the prayers, contemplations and listening as if you are standing before God.

✢   In reciting the chorus and the tunes, it is not allowable to raise your voice over the others or be different from them in the tune.

✢   It is appropriate to come to church in decent clothes worthy of the house of God. Also, those who are receiving communion, they must take off their shoes, and women to cover their hair and do not put makeups.

✢   It is not permissible to leave the church except after hearing the final blessing from the priest, especially on days of Holy Mass.

✢   You must come early to the church, the Lord says, *"And those who seek me diligently will find me."(Prov 8:17)*.

✢   It is assumed that who will partake in communion must attend the early raising of incense (Matins) or at least at the presentation of the offertory and hearing of the absolution of the servants.

✢   It is improper to crowd together during communion or when taking (The Holy Bread).

but to go forward in order, giving preference to one another.

136 - Righteous in His Own Eyes

✢   The problem of Job was being a righteous man and he knows of himself that he is upright. The Bible said about him that, *" ... he was righteous in his own eyes." (Job 32:1)*. So, perhaps for this reason, his known adversity brought upon him.

The ordeal remained with Job when he was righteous in his own eyes, but it was taken away when he said to the Lord, *"Behold I am vile: what shall I answer you? I lay my hand over my mouth." (Job 40:4)*. Also, *"Therefore I have uttered what I did not understand, things too wonderful for me, which I did not know ... therefore I abhor myself and repent in dust and ashes." (Job 42:3 & 6)*.

And when he repented in dust and ashes, the ordeal was lifted.

✢   **The Bible said, *"And lean not on your own understanding." (Prov 3:5)***. It also said, *"Do not be wise in your own opinion." (Rom 12:16)*. And, *"Answer a fool according to his folly, lest he be wise in his own eyes." (Prov 26:5)*.

✢   God wants us not to be wise in our own eyes, therefore he asked us to get discipleship and counselling. It is said,

"Those who are without guide, fall like tree leaves."

He also asked us to obey and consult the grown-ups, like the parents, the spiritual guides, especially the confession fathers as well as the elderly who have experience of the matured.

In order not to be wise in your own eyes, consult others, and in order not to be righteous in your own eyes, remember your sins.

The upright in his own eyes does not accept blame from anyone and sees himself always right. He tries to justify or find excuses for all his mistakes and never admits that he made a mistake. Therefore he falls in pride, stubbornness, obstinacy and argument.

He abides by his mistakes, does not change it because he does not admit it. In the meantime, he loses God's help and His grace might abandon him, so he falls down to feel his weakness.

137 - Why Do We Pray?

We pray in compliance with an order or carrying out a duty. **NO, because prayer is an expression of the love in one's heart towards God**. The righteous person loves God, and through his love for Him, he enjoys talking with Him, the same as a friendly relation between you and a dear friend; you talk together, speak of any subject mainly you enjoy talking with him.

David the Prophet is a practical example of the prayer of love. The Lord says: *"As the deer pants for the water brooks, so pants my soul for you, O God. My soul thirsts for God. When shall I come and appear before God." (Ps. 42:1-3).* He loves God and pants for Him, so he prays.

Therefore if we pray, that is because we feel this love towards God, and while the prayer seems a burden to us, we spend hours talking with our friends without boredom because there is love between us.

Prayer therefore means love. it is a relation with God; it is holding fast to the Lord; it is lifting the heart and mind to God.

There are persons who only pray to seek something from God; if there is nothing to ask for they do not pray as if the personal benefit is the motive for such relation with God! Those are rebuked by St. Basil in his saying [If you stand to pray, do not begin your prayer seeking something, lest it is thought that you pray only because of what you require]. Be sure that all your needs will come to you without seeking them and let your prayer be for love and not a petitionary one.

What did the Lord Jesus ask for when He prayed? He used to spend the whole night in prayer. He does not need anything as everything is in His hands. Isn't He who said," *All things that the Father has are mine." (John 16:15)* then, His prayer was an expression of the love between Him and the Father.

When a person loves God, he loves His Kingdom *"But seek first the Kingdom of God and his righteousness" (Matt 6:33).* With these supplications the Lord's Prayer begin : "Hallowed be your name. Your Kingdom come. You will be done. Give us day by day our daily bread". The heavenly bread which is for our eternal future, the spiritual bread - Your Body and Blood - give us today. It is a supplication based on love. O Lord give us Yourself as we nourish on You. Give us Your sweet words because we live by every word that proceeds from the mouth of God.

Now brother, if you have not yet reached the prayer which is full of love, seek from God what you need: Be frank with God, open your heart to Him. And if such love is not in you, pray that God may give it to you. Say to Him constantly, "Grant me that I love you Lord."

✛ ✛ ✛

138 - What is Suitable

It is difficult to say the same words to everyone. As each person has what suits him and fits for his purpose.

You might need a certain practice today, but might need its opposite tomorrow or even after one hour.

Perhaps you need not to talk, while on another occasion, it is important that you speak, and you feel in your depth that you will be judged on your silence, if you hold your tongue.

A person who is not good with words, or his talk is understood or interpreted differently to what it is meant for a practice of silence is good for such a person. Another person who is asked to testify: if he ceases to talk, his silence is considered a sin.

Therefore, do not read all what is written and carry it out without thinking! but take what suits you and leave the rest to others.

A person, desperate of his salvation, might come to you; and you have to comfort him, explain to him that all his sins are nothing next to God's mercy and love.

If you see a person who exploits God's patience and turns it to inattention, then you talk to him about the ugliness of sin and the fairness of God. Here, you repeat the saying of the Apostle, *"Therefore the goodness and severity of God ... " (Rom 11:22).*

This means there is a time for goodness and a time for severity.

And the wise person uses each in the situation which deems fit.

Gentleness has its time and firmness is necessary at times.

A wise person does not use firmness when it needs gentleness, and gentleness when firmness is a must. His life will not be one without the other; as the perfect personality combines both.

And you, in your life, see many dispositions and numerous cases, and with such contrarieties you need wisdom to study the case and select what it fit for it; firmness or gentleness, silence or talk.

And when you read, read wisely and selectively as deemed suitable for your nature and circumstances.

139 - Exercises on Self-Control

During the period of fasting it is appropriate that you practise self-control as well as the control of your body.

✢   Self-control clearly shows when you keep yourself from something you desire or be affected with, so you do not submit to a certain feeling or internal motive but you control yourself. And the wise man said, "He who rules over himself better than who rules over a city."

✢   As an example, you can try to control yourself at the time of anger and control your inner heart from spite, rage and hatred, and control your tongue from conviction, fury, nervousness and harsh words.

✢   Also you can control yourself over rage, hastiness and rashness and try to be calm; do not speak or give your opinion fast. Do not interrupt others or pronounce a decision unless you are sure it is right.

✢   You can control yourself over any desire that comes into your heart and you long for doing it, do not submit to every desire but restrain your feelings, instincts, wishes, and impulses. Do not make your desires dominate over you but you master over it and bring it under the power of the mind and soul.

✣   Also control yourself in defending your honour or revenging for yourself and remember the saying of the Apostle, "We then who are strong ought to bear the scruples of the weak." (Rom 15:1).

✣   Control yourself with regard to your thoughts; if you were thinking improperly or in trivials, try to stop it or change it to another course.

✣   Control your senses especially your hearing and sight; do not allow yourself to hear or see something indecent.

✣   Control yourself at the time of prayer so that you do not wander or stand without reverence before God.

✣   Try to control yourself with regard to time; do not waste it at pleasures when your time is more valuable.

If you have controlled yourself completely, you have succeeded in your fasting.

140 - You and the Truth

God is the truth. He said of Himself, *"I am the way, the truth and the life." (John 14:6).* He also said, *"And you shall know the truth, and the truth shall make you free." (John 8:32).* The Bible said of the Holy Spirit, *"the Spirit of truth." (John 15:26).*

Therefore, if you walk in the way of truth, you are in God's way and if you say the word of truth, you are telling the word of God.

If you keep back from the truth, in thought, tongue or in deed, you are departing from God.

Some turn away from the truth because of ignorance; and those are the less far. By consciousness and knowledge they return to the truth as long as the heart is sound from inside.

Others turn away from the truth or say the untruth for fear of people, or being shy of them, or becoming weak before them or to flatter them. They need their hearts to be purified.

Some say the untruth to cover themselves like those who conceal their mistakes by lies or insincerity. Undoubtedly those need repentance, as well as to get rid of the sins they committed.

Some say the untruth to side with a friend whom he wants to protect, or as a resentment to a person whom he dislikes. They are like those who bear false witness or trump up charges to hurt others.

Therefore, hatred can turn man away from, the truth, also the wrong love keeps him away from the truth too.

The spiritual person is an upright person, gives everyone his right without injustice or partiality.

Also the spiritual person is fair, even with himself, he does not make compliments at the expense of the truth.

He who loves the truth does not submit half the facts in a deceiving way but tells the truth, the whole truth.

I wonder in which category do you place yourself?

141-Yours or Others Mistakes

People's view of wrong and right , its direction and judgement, differ from person to another according to the contrition or pride of heart.

A humble person concentrates his search on his personal mistakes, and if he blames anyone, he will only blame himself.

But the unlowly will be only preoccupied with the wrongs of others occupies all his thoughts, enthusiasm and all his attention and it might also occupy all his time and energy.

He makes himself a judge over people, to control and judge, and becomes fond of the judicial position, so installs himself judge and pronounce his sentences.

If he finds no wrongs in the others, he imagines it but his suspicion, doubt, mistrust in people, his heart's readiness to listen to what hurts others, no matter how it is untruthful !

He might think that his condemnation of the others on what he sees wrong in them, puts him is a higher level over them, as if he understands what they do not understand, and therefore he is more in thinking, understanding, handling and disposing!

And in all this, he forgets himself. He always censures and cannot accept the blame.

He reproves and cannot accept reproach, criticises and cannot accept criticism.

His own self is without sin, perfect in his eyes. **Therefore it is difficult for the unlowly to repent! Why he repents and he sees no wrong in himself?!**

It is difficult for the unlowly to accept advice. What people understand more than him so that they can give him advice.

The trial which happened to the faithful Job, because *" ... he was righteous in his own eyes." (Job 32:1).*

That is why our teacher the Apostle St. Paul says, *"Do not be wise in your own opinion." (Rom 12:16).*

Solomon the Wise says, *" ... and lean not on your own understanding. Do not be wise in your own eyes." (Prov 3: 5 & 7).*

Happy is the person who condemns himself in everything, who concerns himself in his eternity not by judging people.

142 - How?

It is not important in your life to pray, but what is really important : how to pray ?

Is your prayer a mere repetition of words or it is a real, deep relation with God, which makes you feel the joy of His presence with you, and that you talk to a tangible being, confident that you are standing before Him.

Therefore, it is not the words of the prayer, but as much as what you realise from its understanding and depth, and as much as the mixed spiritual feelings which prove that you mean what you say.

Ask yourself, especially during this holy period of fasting, How to pray? Do you feel that your prayer has ascended to above, and went in the presence of God, and that you heard, in your heart, a special response to it ??

Is your prayer filled with love, in such a manner that you are urged by this love to pray, not because of any obligation.

Is your heart - with all its feelings, desires and affections - tied with God during prayer ? And not like those about whom the Lord said, " *These people honour me with their lips, but their heart is far from me.*" *(Matt 15:8).*

Is your prayer filled with reverence and penance too?.

During which you realise to whom you are talking. He is the unlimited in all His perfections, the Almighty, the Creator, to whom all the knees bow, what in heaven and what on earth. Before Him you are only dust, but because of His extreme humility, He called you son.

Does your prayer have the spirit of faith ?

Do you say your prayer with all concentration?

Is your prayer far from the self and is concentrated on God?

As much as possible you try to concentrate on God; His good attributes which capture your heart; His Kingdom, heaven, angels, promises, companionship, love.

And if you pray, you wish not to stop but to continue praying forever and your life becomes a prayer.

143 - Hope (2)

Since the first sin and before the eviction of our fore parents from paradise, God granted them the hope of salvation and told them that the woman's seed will crush the serpent's head. This was the beginning of hope.

The story of Mary Magdalene gives us an example of hope. This woman, out of whom the Lord cast seven demons, became a great saint and He entrusted her with the announcement of His Resurrection to His disciples. She was also with the Virgin Mary at the cross.

Also the example of Jonah the Prophet gives us the same hope.

Who ever thought that a person who was swallowed by a great fish, kneels to God in the belly of the fish and says, *"I will look again towards your holy temple." (Jon 2:4).*

The above two examples remind us of the three men who were cast in the burning fiery furnace, and Daniel in the lion's den. all are examples of hope.

There is no impossible in the life with God. There is hope whatever the sin is, whatever the troubles are and whatever difficult the case is.

In the spiritual life, how nice are the sayings about hope in the Bible :

" ... all things are possible to him who believes." (Mark 9:23).

"I can do all things through Christ who strengthens me." (Phil 4:13).

If you are fought confronted with hopelessness about your personal abilities, you will not be fought about God's power.

If you are not able to , God can:

Even if you are not seeking Him, He seeks you as He sought the prodigal son and the lost coin. He stands and knocks at your door to open for Him. How great is this hope that God is seeking you.

Satan, in keen insistence, does not lose hope to destroy the most saintly and continues fighting him. How more becomes our hope in God's salvation of sinners.

God gave us hope in incidents mentioned in the Bible, the numerous miracles like the resurrection of the dead, even the one who has been dead for four days.

The greater war by which Satan fights us is hopelessness.

✢ ✢ ✢

144 - The Holy Spirit in Your Life

What is your relationship with the Holy Spirit since you were anointed with the Holy Chrism (Myroun) after your baptism ?

Do you feel your body is the temple of the Holy Spirit and the Holy Spirit of God dwells and works in you ?

Did you enter in communion with the Holy Spirit which the priest mentions in the blessing prayer?

Does the Spirit of God partake in every deed ?

Or you work alone without the Spirit of God, independent with your opinion, will, disposal and personal desires ?

Does the work of the Spirit give you special warmth, either in your prayers or contemplations, service, or your love to God, His church and kingdom?

Are you able to carry out the commandment of the Apostle which says, " ... *be filled with the Spirit." (Eph. 5:18).*

Does the Spirit of God speak with your tongue as it was said, *"For it is not you who speak, but the Spirit of your Father who speaks in you ?" (Matt 10:20).* If it is so, certainly your words will have power and effect on the hearts of your listeners

Or do you talk by yourself and the Spirit does not open your mouth ?

Do you have the fruits of the Spirit about which the Apostle St. Paul talked in (Gal 5:22) when he said, *"But the fruit of the Spirit is love, joy, peace, long-suffering, kindness, goodness, faithfulness, self-control."* Either your life bears no fruit or you wish for the gifts of the Holy Spirit without having the fruit of the Spirit ?!

Do you sometimes feel that *you "grieve the Holy Spirit of God." (Eph. 4:30)* with certain disposals which do not agree with the Holy Spirit which dwells in you.

Do you *"quench the Spirit" (1 Thess 5:19)* with the life of lukewarmness and lack of response to the work of the Spirit in you ?

Would you re-evaluate the extent of your relationship with the Holy Spirit and then ask :

Is your life a spiritual life ? Are your words spiritual ?

145 - The Firm Line

What troubles people most in their spiritualities is the lack of firmness.

Like a person who repents, or assumes he repented, confesses and receives communion, then he returns to his sin as before without firmness in his repentance, his feelings of regret are not firm, also his desire to live with God.

Those who lead that way, they have no constant relationship with His love or kingdom, but they falter between two opinions.

One day they worship God in the tabernacle of meeting and another day they worship the golden calf. They walk with God for months under the cloud, and at another time they murmur, cry and say, " Oh, we stayed in the land of Egypt, we sat by the pots of meat."

They eat the Passover with Christ and agree with the chief priests to betray him to them.

They say to the Lord, "Even if we have to die with you", and after hours they deny Him three times before a servant girl.

The factor of instability troubles the spiritual life and weakens its strength if it continued like that.

There are many reasons for the lack of firmness in the spiritual life:

It might be because the spiritual life is not based on love or it is mere formalities from the outside which has no foundation in the depth of the soul.

The reason might be an unforeseen fear if the relationship with God - the time of which has already passed - or a temporary warmth faded after some time, or by a provisional effect the causes of which were eliminated.

It might be that the relationship with God has started without ending the relation with sin, or that its causes still remain.

It might be a shaken personality, or liable to inclination, easily affected to the right or left, attracted to the spiritualities sometimes or to the worldliness.

The instability does not help at all to grow spiritually.

How can a person grow if he sometimes goes backwards, falls and rises, rises and falls without firmness ?!

Therefore, the Lord says, "Abide in me, and I in you." He seeks this firmness and says, "Abide in my love."

✛ ✛ ✛

146 - Sacrifice

The love which does not sacrifice is a barren love, without fruit.

Love is a productive mother that gives birth to numerous virtues such as compassion and affection, a word of encouragement and a word of consolation, attention and care, forgiveness and seeking the salvation of the soul. This is the spiritual love.

Perhaps the most distinguished quality in love is sacrifice.

This is the big difference between love and lust. Love always seeks to give and lust always seeks to take.

Lust seeks to take because it is concentrated around the self, but love, as the Apostle said," *... does not seek its own."*

Love that does not sacrifice is not a true love.

Love sacrifices everything, does not keep anything from whom it likes, no matter how this thing is precious or essential to it.

The best a loving person can do is to sacrifice himself, and the Lord said, *"Greater love has no one than this, to lay down his life for his friends." (John 15:13)*. This was shown in depth on the cross.

The crucified Jesus is a sacrifice of love. The Bible said, *"For God so loved the world that he gave his only begotten Son, that whoever believes in him should not perish but have everlasting life." (John 3:16).*

During the Passion Week, many contemplate the passion of Christ. Christ's passion is merely a natural result of his love. Love here is the origin and passion is the outside appearance.

Would we contemplate His love which He has shown in His passion?

The candle melts to give light to others, it also sacrifices itself for the sake of others; we put candles before the icons of the saints it is a symbol.

Also the incense seed burns in fire to give sweet smell which ascends to God. It is a delightful burnt offering to God, and it is a symbol.

147 - Resurrection is a Spring of Hope

Man triumphed in hundreds of fields except death. Before death, man stood helpless and hopeless.

Then came the resurrection to give the first victory over death :

The Apostle says in a challenge, "O Death, where is your sting?"

Then, hope in the eternal life enters man's heart and fills it with joy, that he will not perish or come to an end.

Also, the church receives those who pass away with the beautiful chant "it is not death to your servants but it is a transition."

The chanter also says in the psalm, *"The right hand of the Lord does valiantly; the right hand of the Lord is exalted ... I shall not die, but live, and declare the works of the Lord." (Ps. 118:16/17)*

Victory over death gave hope to triumph over all other things, because who overcomes the powerful certainly can handle those who are weaker than him.

Therefore, through victory over death, the morale of the children of God has risen, and our teacher St. Paul said, "I can do all things through Christ who strengthens me."

Also, before man there was no difficulty, no impossible, but "all things are possible to him who believes".

The spirit of the resurrection spread out its hope on everything.

Before any difficulty or problem stands the picture of the Lord who resurrected from the dead to give hope that after death there is life, and after darkness there is light, and there is a solution to every problem.

That is how the children of God lived *"Rejoicing in hope"***(Rom. 12;12).** They see that everything around them *"Even though he dies, he shall live"* that is why they *"should not sorrow as others who have no hope"*

Here ends the grieves of Gethsemane and the passion of Golgotha, the suspicion and fear of the upper room. But the remains the picture of the bright angel before the empty tomb to announce the Resurrection.

148 - Envy Of The Devil

In the Holy Mass we say in the Prayer of Reconciliation "You destroyed death which was introduced into the world by the envy of the devil".

We see that Satan envies every good and successful deed, because goodness and success are against his satanic plan to resist the Kingdom of God on earth, either in relation to individuals or groups.

The devil always labours to fight the children of God and his labour is in vain.

When he finds out that he toiled in vain with no result, his hatred and envy to the children of God increases. His wars become more fierce, and after they are fought in secret, they turn out openly and without shame pressing on the children of God without mercy. But God will not let " *... the sceptre of wickedness shall not rest on the land allotted to the righteous."* *(Ps. 125:3).*

Therefore, in every good deed you expect the envy of the devils but do not fear them.

At the ordination of a new monk, a chapter from the Book of Joshua Bin Sirach is read to him, which says, "Son, if you engage in the service of your God, prepare yourself for all trials"

With the same meaning, we read in the sayings of St. Aughiris to the devoted monk "If you start the holy prayer, be prepared for whatever comes to you". He means be ready for the wars of the devil which he declared on you because of your holy worship.

How poor is the devil who spends his life in envy, hatred and war !

His envy does not harm the sons of God, but in fact it harms him and increases his eternal punishment. Also, such envy gives him more grief, sadness, distress and trouble. Any harm the devil tries to impose on the sons of God is an external harm, unreal and does not affect their eternity; how quick God saves them.

Satan might fight the sons of God directly as it happened with the righteous Job, and he might fight them through his human helpers.

In both ways his envy will end in vain because the grace of God intervenes and stops his evil deed. God stay and all his enemies disperse, all those hate his Holy Name will flee.

Even if Satan showed success at first he will surely fail at last.

When Satan envied Job the righteous, it seemed that he succeeded in his plan and triumphed over Job, he destroyed his house, killed all his children, struck him with painful boils from the sole of his foot to the crown of his head, made his friends reproach and disgrace him, but the whole matter ended to the contrary; the Lord restored Job's losses and gave him twice as much as he had before.

Satan is tormented by his own envy before the sons of God strike him.

149 - The Confession Father

✢   He is the person when you see him you remember God, His rights and commandments.   You also remember your promises before God.

✢   He is the one who can change your life to better with his deep spiritual effect as well as his knowledge, relation with God and good example.

✢   He is an oasis in the desert of your life where you rest and think of God, not the oasis or the rest.

✢   He is not a bridge you cross to reach the other side, but he is a plane which flies you over all coasts and takes you to your target.

✢   He is the one who can make you cry and so you rejoice in your weeping more than all the fun and laughs.   Sometimes, he can be harsh on you, or it appears to you that he is harsh, however, such hardness could be more tender and gentle than the kindness which makes you lose your life.

✢   He is not the father who considers you a child all your life, carries you on his shoulders, guides you in all matters, but he is the wise conductor who carries you for some time until you learn wisdom and distinction, until you can stand on your feet and carry others on your shoulders and teach them.

✛	The true confession father does not toil to bind you to his heart, love and obedience, but he binds you to the heart, love and obedience of God. But, he tries to disappear so that God appears in you. He does not consider himself the owner of the vineyard, but only a steward sent by God to his vineyard to prune that it may bear more fruit.

✛	The confession father is not a master who always ask for obedience, submission and respect, but as a father he is full of love and affection. He is not a tie around your will, but he is the person who trains your freedom in the love of God.

✛	The confession father is a carrier of sins and takes them off your head and put them on the head of Christ who bore the sins of the whole world. He is a person who lays his hand on your head then you feel that a heavy burden has been removed. He is a source of peace, announcer of good news; the forgiveness of God. He explains God's love and makes an opening of hope to lighten the darkness of your life.

✛	The confession father is the practical example of every virtue; you take from his life and his doctrine, and benefit from his manner of life not only from his guidance.He is the person whom whenever you see, your spiritual passion and love to God increases.

150 - A Pleasant Word

Your words often define your relations with people.

With a word you can please a person, and with another you can sadden, anger, agitate or convert him to an enemy !

You might say a word, unintentionally, quickly, then you spend many years to handle its consequences and perhaps you fail. So, let your word be pleasant to the ears of others.

How sweet was the saying of the Angel to the shepherds, *"for behold, I bring you good tidings of great joy which will be to all people." (Luke 2:10)*. Also, the Bible said, ***"How beautiful are the feet of those who bring glad tidings of good things." (Rom 10:15)***.

How beautiful is the word of blessing and the word of prayer. It is a pleasant word.

The weeping Hannah heard it through the mouth of Eli the priest, so she went her way and her face was no longer sad.

How pleasant is the saying of the Lord Jesus to the sinful woman, who was caught in the very act, *" ... neither do I condemn you; go and sin no more." (John 8:11)*. It is a resolution of forgiveness which pleased the woman's heart.

The word of "forgiveness" is pleasant to the ears, and the word of "love" is also desirable to hear.

The ear can entirely distinguish the word filled with emotion and hearty feelings and can point out its truth and actual expression.

The word of encouragement and praise is also a pleasant word. It is said in the Bible, *"Comfort the faint-hearted" (1 Thess 5:14)..*

Encouragement gives confidence to the soul, comforts and makes it feel that its speaker is involved and following its work and pleased with it. Also its efforts are not wasted but appreciated.

The word of appreciation pleases even the grown-ups; we make them feel our support, ideal inclination and thinkable concord.

How nice is a word of encouragement said by a doctor to his patient or a professor to his student, even how nice is a simple smile.

The cheerful sweet face is also loved by people.

People want features that give them relief and overspread quietness and peace in their hearts with a pleasant word out of lips which drip honey.

✦✦✦